T0023518

SAINT FRIEND

Books by Carl Adamshick

Curses and Wishes (2011)
Saint Friend (2014)
Receipt: Poems (2017)
Birches (2019)

SAINT FRIEND

POEMS BY
Carl Adamshick

Carnegie Mellon University Press
Pittsburgh 2019

Library of Congress Control Number: 2018940311
ISBN 978-0-88748-643-2
Copyright © 2014 by Carl Adamshick
All rights reserved
Printed and bound in the United States of America

10 9 8 7 6 5 4 3 2 1

Saint Friend was originally published by McSweeney's, San Francisco,
in 2014. The Carnegie Mellon University Press cover is a variation of the
original cover art (and frontispiece) by Ian Huebert.

First Carnegie Mellon University Press Classic Contemporaries Edition,
October 2019.

CONTENTS

LAYOVER

They keep paging Kenneth Koch at the airport.
Someone should let the announcer know
he is dead, that there is no city he can go to,
that no one is expecting him. Once, I applied
to be a horse. The mirror of night had shed
its clothes, and I needed to be something
that mattered. I needed to scrape my brown
flank against the bark of a ponderosa.
My friends have moved away. They sleep
in places I've never been. And here we are.
It's the most miraculous thing. We walk
over counter-weighted bridges in love
with snow tumbling through their lights.
The terminal's long glass walls dark at this hour.
I feel we live similar lives, only the time zone
and language different. In the cab,
on the way, I saw what was real and humane
in front of a pub: a bicycle leaning
against a thin trunk, lights strung in trees
reflected in shop windows. I loved the way
they loved out there at dusk. Tables littered
with wallets and phones, hats, a beer divided
between two glasses, someone showing someone
a new shirt, sheltered in the camber of voices.
I thought nothing will ever be easier or better.
We will not rise. It is too late.
The year we write on our checks too high
to ever expect anything to be different.
We will always live here, ancient and new.

These are the people we are. Saint friend,
carry me when I am tired and carry yourself,
let's keep singing the songs we don't live by.
Let's meet tomorrow. We don't have to wait
until the holidays. The distance is long,
but it is nothing. Remember when we lived together,
when we kissed, when we talked about fog
on the morning lake and the markings
we wanted on our graves?
The city is lit. I'm up in the air.
It is yes until I die. And when I die,
I want to be paged once a day in an airport
somewhere on this earth, so people
will think I am just running late or lost,
will think I am in transit, sad about the last
embrace, or sad to leave the city of snow
and bridges, or eager to land, to walk
the small wooden streets of my house.
One city, once a day. I wish that for everyone.
An unknown elegy briefly filling the ears
of strangers. I picture my friends dead, nightly,
because I can't see them, because
I can't hear them. I want to love them
enough. I want to dress the wound of their absence
enough. I thought I would be the dead one,
stretched out on the coffin of my bed,
the white bull come to mourn one of its disciples,
its head of fourteen stars, but my body
keeps telling me it's my friends

who have vanished, that they will no longer tip
a dollar for a few pints of porter
or stand in a kitchen full of words and laughter.
I tell my body I will keep their memories
and my body says: *they will be anchors.*
Then I will collect their shadows
and my body says: *you are not a reliquary.*
Their eyes are stitched shut, their mouths are stitched shut,
and all the verbs surrounding their names
are dead verbs. I don't want to hold my body.
I don't want to hold my body or listen to it.
From above, the clouds of Stockholm
are a tilled white field and from below
they are a low gathering of gray letting go
their misery. Tomorrow I see the Vasa,
a ship inlaid with so much gold it sank
a few meters into its journey. It was raised
from the water some three hundred and thirty
years after its descent into the silt
and had a museum built around it.
The voyage sallied forth in all its beauty
and finally became a treasure. Just like
your life or mine with its quiet, dark room
holding a golden boat. A destination
different than expected. So many paths.
So many apologies. So much gratitude.
Luggage rides the carousel turning
with a repetitive clank. The floor shines
like a museum's. Art often seems

a kind of funeral. The important things
we leave. I half expect to see bouquets
under the paintings. I never much believed
in the muse, never much believed my belief
was carried too far out into the world.
In the gallery, doesn't everything speak
to relations, hasn't everything always spoken
to relations, to the smallest gesture?
Let the muse make whatever needs to be made,
let the muse tend the fire. Your whole body
is curled like an ear I wanted to talk
into all evening. Your hand, a ring
of articulated keys. I want that moment
when we climb down the bright ladder
of ecstasy, when our breath comes back,
when everything is alive, present
in the moment with nothing to wait for,
nothing to worry over, only the need to rise
into the beauty that is. The folded clothes,
the interior of a suitcase with its personal logic
being carried on elevators and escalators,
the moving walkway. Being alone
in a theater and seeing the latch, handle,
and the old stickers stuck on the leather
helping the narrative along. Then
an open umbrella floating on the park's
pond. The screen holding all that blue light.
I always thought death would be like traveling
in a car, moving through the desert,

the earth a little darker than sky at the horizon,
that my life would settle like the end of a day
and I would think of everyone I ever met,
that I would be an invisible passenger,
quiet in the car, moving through the night,
forever, with the beautiful thought of home.
Like when my mother calls from the far side
of history saying: *honey, everything brings*
everything back. A red-barked tree applauds
the day. Summer is warm and light so late.
The bruise which was hers. The map
she folded and gave to me. I think
of her in the quiet house. In her death
I see her eyes closed in prayer. Her hand
that was never a star. Her foot that was kissed
but never a bridge. Her heart that was never
anything but a heart. I see her smoking
her first cigarette, hip and shoulder against brick.
I see her laughing in the blue car
as it crosses the border. I touch a picture
of my brother, born in early February.
I remember the dream where she held a stone
like a book of fables. I see the year of my birth,
my mouth searching for her body.
She often says: *stars are cheap glass*
held in burnt tinfoil, space the unliked cousin
to nothingness. I spent my life avoiding my life.
It's easier than you might think.
Time is a younger sister hiding her anger.

I don't want to hold my body,
the minor keys or the dissonant chords.
There is space in here for you.
There is more time than you can imagine.
The purple tulips buck in the wind
as if their white roots were a cavalry
marching. Approaching the mountain
they are swallowed first by its shadow,
then by its mystery. I'm confident
there are different ways to think within
my own thinking. One illustration
of this is to look at a handful of bubbles
from a bath. Across the concourse, a plane
comes to a stop at gate F7. Soon, people
will come through the door at the end
of the hall. It's one thing one second,
another thing another second.
The chess clock counts forty-seven minutes
before a rook is moved one square
to the left. It's in the way you listen
to the outward flow of another's resistance,
and to your own. You cannot lie.
Each person watches the same accretion.
None of us language, none of us silent
to the way days happen. The blunt head
of a pawn is stuck in the mesh of pieces,
in the beautiful contention to survive.
Sun warms the window, half the globe.
Wind pushes through trees clustered with acorns.

Cars line the gray-pocked street. It's so peaceful
at eleven AM, I understand light as a thing
we breathe. Last week, the doctor let me
use the otoscope to look into her ear. Hidden
in the hollow, I saw a small cataracted eye,
an eye not meant to see or be seen, translating
everything that comes to it. Like my mother
I don't know how to live. If only I could travel
fast enough and far enough to see what has happened.
The evening is trying to slip through a seam
in the horizon. The moment I believe bats
sleep in their cave like a dying black fire, I know
I've begun my walk back to the beginning.

PACIFIC

> I was sure of it that night.
> —Amelia Earhart

It was Valentine's Day.
I bent to the stranger's scar.

The beds were filled
and the moon laying its light on men
abandoned

to their immediate selves
was half, and seen through

a welt of tree limbs
that opened onto the night.

It was inflamed, segmented
as a tapeworm, running the length
of his neck

before going into his gown.
I lifted the cotton to see

if it settled in the hairs of his chest.

◆

One could disappear in this,

above rainfall and cloud, oceanic mist.
Every half-hour

I am to crank the cable,
let it out in an arc under the plane
and radio in

what the instruments read.
It is all water—

stars are setting
in the expansive light-tipped migration of it.

One is bound to think
anything in this humming shell
of propulsion.

I dismiss most as thought,
and the rest becomes real.

◆

They shoveled a trench that filled with snow.
The butt of a rifle

struck the bridge of a nose,
a bayonet gouged a cheek, tore

the inside of a throat. Some froze,
fingers and feet amputated.

In the hospital
I'd seen them as kites
caught above the current,

aching to come down
to their lives.

On the fields,
they saw each other,

gaping eyes, rictus of brutality.

◆

I'm not sure they hear me.

I tell them I'm getting tired
of this fog.

All that crackle in their ears
and mine
and I'm not sure it matters.

I can always drop down and find a gray
vessel in the dark swells.

8 hours out and up
and there's no way I can miss.

8000 feet, 135 miles an hour
and nothing but me, my memory

working like a rhumb line back to my birth,
which must've been like this—

water, flying, an expectant crowd.

◆

On Sundays I took a streetcar to the stables,
pockets filled with sugar and carrot

for a brindled mare
I'd ride over the cold muck of new thaw.

The men were getting to me,
none of them looked guilty.
It was as if you could love them

in their laughter.
I took myself in, wore myself cautiously

around the theological college,
around the patients.

What they did was common.

I listened to the distant factories
on nights I thought of holding a soldier

as his ache and cry came like milk.

◆

Money was my father's tonal center,
the place his mouth always returned to.

The day after I broke his bottle
in the basement sink
we walked a muddy field

to see an aspen
struck by lightning.
Severed four feet up the trunk,

its crown of curling leaves
convinced my father to tell me

he had no purpose
or income.

He was an inventor of one thing.

He drank and rummaged
in the cleft of his misgivings.

◆

We were up late drinking lemon water,
biting into soft biscuits,

navigating. The night loosed. A needle

sank to its groove, bridge
was dealt with a red deck,

1936 was a room with two soft lamps.
I'll always slip into that scene
for reassurance.

When it was my turn to talk
about fathers I said:

Hawaii

is now one short flight
to volcanoes and birds

you've never seen—
where the land grows before your eyes.

◆

How he thinks of her: all day turning.
From his office

he sees a field of lupine
he could gather and give her.

The job is nothing compared to his days
in wheat
listening to his father
mumble pieces of a sermon,

nothing to the torrid shoveling of coal.

On the fourth afternoon of marriage,
he flops on the bed
which is not his,
in the house which is

not his.

◆

My father must have felt like nowhere.
There is no anger or malice

in equations, science's polemics
are clear—

proof and uncertainty.

This is where family begins
to tear
open in me like an orange,

like the moment you know
you've given the wrong gift.

My father was abandoned,
died in debt.

When I think of him
it is with pity, the emotion

a parent most fears.

◆

My traveling possessions:
a raft and a hatchet.

I would survive
maybe a week with my supply
of tomato juice and chocolate.

If I couldn't retrieve the raft
from behind the fuselage,

if the Lockheed went in
nose first and fast,

I'd wait
and take one heavy breath of water.

My lungs would burst, my head stop.
And my life
in the compartment of its body,

would dance a slowtime
to the elemental bottom.

◆

I wonder what it is like to fill
with another life.
Before me

my mother lost a child. Could I live

through a loss like that,
could I sit one morning with sunlight
filtering through burdock

and rise and wake
a beloved
and say I am pregnant,

and then through the months
dream of eye color and sex,

only to never?

How would I do that?

◆

I am too close to the ocean, too close
and losing
my senses to the hours.

I want to believe
in morality, that action is governable
and correctable,

but I find myself listening

and when I listen
I find I can't judge reason.

The clouds well with light—
gravid water
dissipates into morning.
I'm bearing in on California.

I punctuate the dawn, replete, volant.

◆

It makes sense with my parents,
with me, you do anything
not to suffer,

you do anything to have love.

It's the tension of nature—
little offerings, little apologies.

But it's different with the soldiers,
they volunteer—

they are willing to not be loved.

They are the other car,
the one you see passing.

◆

We did what we wanted—
then conspired.

Autumn sweaters, mittens, scarves, hats,
crepuscular Missouri, and a leaf
in my sister's hand.

Placing my reliance in the life of another,
trusting her

not to fold, not to cower
in mother's wool.

And then the lying, that gush of pleasure
and the way our lives
overlapped.

I was never closer to anyone,

alive in the secrecy, in the glorious
danger, in the freedom in deceit.

♦

The silence
of an aftermath

ends,
and a serenity invades your body.

It is the solace of a shadow

lost on black water.
The overwhelming sadness in seeing

yourself as human, limited
to one term, is fleeting.

Sound is an extremity
to pain, to the core of silence.

What will be the first thing you say

after the recognition

that you are continuing
without effort?

◆

I need to land, to slip from the crowd,
to recover from this waking.

Once I saw a bed
lifted and lowered on the waves
of an emerald-white sea,

fruit rolling on its mattress
or caught in blue knots of linen.

The basket lashed with twine and chain.

Because it hurt,
it seemed to be a window with one star,
a room where a limb was cauterized,

a place you feel light.

And it seemed you could live once
or you could die a thousand times a second.

NEAR REAL-TIME

February First

I woke in my shallow bed
thinking I want less   quiet
that I would share whatever I had.
But today   I can't sit
oblivious to the world
and drink coffee and toast bread
with you. If we talked about love
death   the time you ate an apple
on the damp library steps
we would be hiding.

February Second

Friend   a friend
says I need
everyday   words
for the administration.
Behind
the mirrors   red
knotted at its throat
history is birthed
as the long hallway reflects us.

February Fourth

Tell me stories of lineage
how you move
from day to day   reasons
knowledge is uncertain   reason
to me. I'll fix jasmine tea
the way you like it
bring raspberries
kumquats   place the cold gems
in your mouth   one
by one. Empty
the world of everything
except this.

February Fifth

I saw you place the spoon on a napkin
turn the kettle off before the whistle
as if it were morning
and you didn't want to wake them.

They are not coming back. Night
has covered your house. You believed
the garden's way   in the customs
of grace. You believed the wind

the rain   the seed and the leaf.
You believed habit was to give
and be given.

February Sixth

Think of the room where you learned
preference   one thing over another.
Think of what you first dismissed

it's like anything you no longer need

alive   beautifully   without you.
Think of an ocean
ending   only to recede
into its restless body.

Think of what you want.
Think of a ditch of dead bodies
covered with lime. Then come to me
and whisper if you can.

February Seventh

There are two paintings
one on top of the other.
There is the life told to you
and the one you understand
know.   There is memory
and you now   now
now as always   an exile
or emigrant within the borders
of your skin.   Tell me again
how you fear people
only get so smart   how the future
will be the same as the past
how the cage of the brain
was locked upon us.

February Eighth

Sunset. We take what we want.
Slaughter. We see in fire
how we are not the enemy.
That's all we ever really wish for,
to be the ones who do the damage.

We've seen teeth
embedded in charred flesh.

We've seen how dirt sticks to brain.
We know this is where language leads
that we are the final

annunciation. Fire is the result
of angering the air.
When we come you will breathe it
our word   our glory.

February Ninth

You will never know life without death.
The sea can churn its babbling mouth
through the night. The sky can rise
until it breaks into space
but you will never know life
without death.

When you are freed   maybe then
the sea will mourn
will lay your body on its shore
and the sky lower itself
as a flower to your chest.

February Tenth

I have an enemy I don't want to conquer
a favorite tree in the park
ten blocks from here. I have a love
I can't express well enough
often enough. The tree is a blue atlas cedar
its needles   in the rain
never look wet.   Growing up
I talked to the road near my house
when it was barren and its straight miles
were buried under an eternity of moonlight.

February Eleventh

                My only wish

is that I die before you
so I don't meet that pain
or court that suffering
or marry that awful hollowness.
So I don't have a child with grief
that will open my breast
and drag a thread of loss
into the infinite pool of air.

February Twelfth

Here is where we make our promises
where I see you living
and want to live too   away
from all the constructs.

I find you continually   experiencing
at the cost of experience. Your bright
uncontrollable name stretched
in a constellation
on the eve of the winter solstice.

If we had any sense
we would be making love.
Our hands   sloppy with it.
Our hands   like a mouth
and our mouths like an eye.
All the necessities
getting confused
in the half-lit darkness.
Our minds sensing the same things
and different things. We should
be thankful   I tell you.
We should enter the house
of gratitude and help cook dinner.

February Thirteenth

I put the back of my wrist
to your dead temple.
The sun is a fist of glass burning
through its own reflection.

If we could see
if we could possibly
make sense of the world.

A desire to place
four fingers of scotch
in the pocket
of a wide-mouthed lowball.

February Fourteenth

Say they found his body
in the shade of a chestnut   carried
him to the closest moving water.
Say they put him in an anchored boat
and watched birds take his flesh.

Say the river froze   the little prow
tilted toward the north bank
and you could see snow on his bowels.

When an Appaloosa trampled
the first yellow tulip   they pulled
him to shore   magnified his bones
in a bed of alcohol
made from a black crescent leaf.
Say they slid sticks into the opening
of his stomach   turned them
to form a star. His tongue
cut with flint   was dyed red.
His teeth pulverized
with mortar and pestle. A girl
filled a cloth boat
with the dust of his mouth
placed his tongue on top
carefully   like her parents
putting her to sleep   lowered the ship
into the world of his stomach
slung it over a branch of the tree
they found him under.

Say you woke to see his skull
wrapped in blue flame
found the elders
under the dried skin   inking
his clean bones   a bundle
of herbs at each of their feet.
Say it was evening
and in the morning they hinged
him back together   laid him

in the center of the feasting table
read his body.
Say they placed a round
of bread in his rib cage
blue eggs and flowers in his pelvis
a bowl of sheep's milk in his blackened skull
dressed him in thorns   rust-colored
chestnut leaves   vines
and mounted him on a dead horse.

February Fifteenth

I thought when you died
something else would go with you
the lime leaf   black currant.
I thought we would skip summer
that the box turtle would become extinct
that we would be   unable   to eat.

Days kept passing. I remember now.
We were drinking red tea.
You were telling me about the stars
and all I could think was how your hat
was blocks away   sitting
on a pile of raked leaves.

February Sixteenth

We walk through a field sick with dead bodies.
We carry chairs. Think
we leave with our chairs. Think   *theater.*
A nest within us holds suffering.

A nest within us understands
beauty as those moments of giving.
Think *the loud killing.* Think *yolk in the skull.*

The trees endure   their structure
like the bones of some magnificent animal.
Think *floating under the spine in the lost museum.*

February Seventeeth

Now that I am empty
I want to feel the weight of life.
Now that I'm alone
I want a room with people.
Now that I'm dressed
for the coffin's slow ride
I want to live as gently as a book.
Now I say   when I have no now.

February Eighteenth

The divers surface with hands
bloodied from the gathering.
The riders a deathchain
on the blue ridge.
Cooks sway in the steam
of the metal hull
and you consider God
a relative.
Bear down. History
comes as a lame bird to battle.

February Nineteenth

It doesn't matter what you do.
It didn't happen
if I hold comfort like a stranger
after a day of work.   After a day
you didn't mean anything.
I won't speak   if content.
It wouldn't matter if I saw the crime
as long as it doesn't touch me
as long as you don't touch me.

February Twentieth

At dinner   a detonation
of grief collapses your face.
I get on my knees

lips pressed to your ear.
Then I'm at the sink
staring at dishes.

Soon we will be
what we can't understand.

It's what we don't
have words for
that grows lonely within us.

February Twenty-First

I have six bodies constantly bleeding
a drowned girl I sleep with in the attic.
It doesn't hurt when you drive by
in your black car with the windows down
a cigarette locked in your lips   staring
like I'm a cheerleader bent to get a nickel.
You come like the others
to scout my wound   wander through

the garden. It's you or someone else.
I've learned it doesn't matter who runs
their fingers over the mantle. They eventually
tire. They eventually want something   else.
They start circling like strays   hate
flitting in their eyes. It's what you become
when you begin losing. An empty bottle.
A chain bolted to the basement wall.
I've held them as they forgot who they are.
I've loved them and have loved the sound
of their breaking   the acknowledgment
that power is not shared.

February Twenty-Second

After the laws and executions
the declarations   the councils
the dogs of an afternoon hunt
after the regnant power drifts apart
like torn cloud   becomes sky
or rain or anything that isn't you
you will retreat home
to the backyard   to yourself.
You will sit with an image of the crown
at the bottom of the teeter-totter.

February Twenty-Third

Two days ago we all
came home from the hospital.
A house is never so quiet
as when its family is sleeping.

To see that child's mouth
cover her nipple
was to see much of my life
fall away   it was to see snow
before it falls
to see mineral
lace its way through rock.

February Twenty-Fourth

You're missing. I lift a pan from a hook
place it over the fire. The expectation
of taste. The quintet of the body
reeling   reveling in talk.

Hours of light and pleasure
as the feast builds   without form
into a style of departure   a ride
a wave. It is to live without living.

Wake at dawn to a table
clean of wine and bone.

February Twenty-Fifth

After dinner we walk
through the neighborhood
everything cut back.

When I was a house
I had a couple
who lost their only child.

The grocery store is empty.
The lot has just a few cars
when the snow begins.

When I was a sparrow
everything became a lyric
in the songbook of the eye.

Two clerks are talking.
From here it looks
as though they are friends.

When I was dead
I couldn't love you.

February Twenty-Sixth

You can go through
heartache   hatred   deceit.
You can stand there softened
by the experience of being
altered by another   knowing
you are within them.
You can get closer. You can shed
your clothes   become small
and walk a path into their bones.
You can spend years devoted
turning their phrases and faceted
moments in the light
and you can enter the diamond
of who they are. And not see
the glinting cut   but be
the tint and hue. So when they weep
you weep. So when they laugh
you laugh. You can be their laughter.

February Twenty-Seventh

I hear women
living in the ground
unable to eat or wash
are waiting.

History doesn't live here.

We are one century
bone thistle loss
laid down with our names
all our instruments muted.

When I was eleven
I tore my wrist on a jagged rock.
The sap red ink seeped
crawled down my arm.
I was scared   reverential
at seeing the thing
that silently kept me alive.

February Twenty-Eighth

A plane will open its belly   drop
its luggage of explosives. The living
will choke   plead. Bullets
will move through flesh as birds through shadow
nest in bone   bathe.
You can imagine
how it could be forgotten   confused.
The length of day will not vary.
Someone will hide in a death mound.
Do not pray it won't happen.

It will   and worse.
Do not hope   hope has killed many.

March Eighteenth

When Blood took our hands
walked us to the orchard
when Blood whispered
I have filled myself with myself
no longer can I hide in the earth
it was not enough. When we found Blood
black and thick within the fruit
it was not enough. When Blood
was in our throats   on our tongues
we still looked at one another
and said *because.*

THE MATHEMATICIAN

She has taken to sleeping late.

Solid, almost vaporous in sheer morning light.
I'm obsessed, after thirty years,
how her mind keeps things,
how her body stores, how the runnels and rills
operate, how they order.

Simon was pulled from her. A birth like theft.

A numb seam opposite her spine,
a bright ridge that reddens
when she sinks into the bath. Her reminder.
A mark more violent
than the navel. This is how you no longer live.

Naked. Unbelievably naked.
I just stare.

A severe meandering. I see her life and then can't
say it. Painstaking and then lost,
serene then helpless.
And when my mind is unable to focus

I get up and look from the other side of the room.

◆

What I do is calculate.

I've always seen the world as numbers,
buildings and trees as factors,
math as a language better suited for explaining
how things work
than the formula of grammar.

The rate of explosions, the intake of air,
the probability of the atmosphere
to ignite. It can be any equation
and I see the solution
as reality etched with numbers.

Her heart could house a cathedral.

◆

She told me her dreams
are water and bone, grief, ash and mold.

She is fifty-four.
Gray strands tangle in the white bedding.
How do you collect the details of her,
the creases by the eye?

Painters could spend months on the curve
of her arm when it's stretched
over her head, hand on the pillow,
armpit exposed.

A thousand sketches before color is contemplated.

In 1910, she spent her summer walking
a cold riverbed buried in noon shade.

She watched her father hang black men
from a trestle, watched her mother watch,
saw her brother playing in the dirt.

I think of her as a fugue,
as relief in metal, as a chamber
comprehending music,
as a monument people touch in winter.

She is on her side,
one knee bent across the other.
The hinge of her elbow. The desk
by the window has a tall,
thin, unlit candle
and a wooden bowl that holds nothing.

How do you understand this in observation?

She is not math.

◆

If I could press my thumb to the arch of her foot
and convince her,

if I could trace the line of her calf, thigh,
hard rise of her hip,
to show her that the living are not monsters,
that we act out of necessity, I would,

but to her,
the guilty live and the dead become sovereign,
exalted, protected from change.

She is in the act of forgetting
why the light was made to overtake their bodies.

◆

We came together like music
that should never be forgotten.

Acute, concerned, coupling

technology and foresight,
we invented whatever was needed.
The sound of a nation
at industry, shaping planes by the thousands.

Around the clock
we riveted, heated, bent a massive undertaking
to our will. It was beauty,
unwavering brilliance,
that sped us to accomplishment.

Time itself is decision.
My life has been in front of her every day.

I recall evenings we lingered in the cool tub
not wanting to wallow
in the burdensome heat,
days we drove to blooming cherry and dogwood.

I know death is a friend

you can feel sorry with,
but she was not blind to my job.

She knew and lived with the recognition
and now cannot claim
to have known, within our days, other days.

It's been five weeks since Hiroshima.
I never wake her.
I don't want this to ruin us.

A MAP TO NOW

I didn't know a woman could vanish
within herself, didn't know
fear would then be her master.

I didn't see the sun under the lindens
of November, or the moon riding
a wet black horse.

I thought my body was mine
until it became a window,
a map anyone could use.

I didn't see the red lights
of the radio tower, or the city park
laded with fog.

The year had slipped out
of its clothes, and midnight
arrived in formal attire,

everyone swayed, held in the music,
sure the turning
of the year

was an entrance into an afterlife
of unlimited sunshine.
We lived.

I tried to explain the sound
within our dreaming
not as the ocean, but street names.

EMILY

It is nice to be without answers
at the end of summer.
Wind lifting leaves from branches.

The moment like something
laid down in childhood
and forgotten about until later,
when stumbled upon, and we think:
this is where it was lost.

The sadness isn't their sadness.
The sadness is the way

they will never unpack the rucksack
of happiness again.

They'll never surface as divers rising
through leagues of joy, through sun
willowing through the waves' carriages.
They will never surface again.

Again and again,
they will never surface.

MICHAEL

I told a friend to celebrate
the end of a love.

I think, I've told him too many things.

His heart has fallen.

He is grieving,
it is not failure hollowing out his bones.

I've seen him on the corner,
the streetlight pushing

a shadow through his spine,
the moonlight laying another one

he could step into if he crossed the lawn.

THOMAS

There is an oar wedged
in your body because
the future can be anything
and anything so vast.
The handle pains your ankle.
The blade looks out through
your lungs onto a warm summer field
singing with insects.
But what makes the oar great
is that it also looks out
from the field to you
stopped on the road.

EVERYTHING THAT HAPPENS
CAN BE CALLED AGING

I have more love than ever.
Our kids have kids soon to have kids.
I need them. I need everyone
to come over to the house,
sleep on the floor, on the couches
in the front room. I need noise,
too many people in too small a space,
I need dancing, the spilling of drinks,
the loud pronouncements
over music, the verbal sparring,
the broken dishes, the wealth.
I need it all flying apart.
My friends to slam against me,
to hold me, to say they love me.
I need mornings to ask for favors
and forgiveness. I need to give,
have all my emotions rattled,
my family to be greedy,
to keep coming, to keep asking
and taking. I need no resolution,
just the constant turmoil of living.
Give me the bottom of the river,
all the unadorned, unfinished,
unpraised moments, one good turn
on the luxuriant wheel.

HAPPY BIRTHDAY

The universe is infinite
and somehow expanding.

If you believe what people say

then you believe each of us is at its center,

and if it's your birthday today,
it will also, somewhere,
be your birthday tomorrow.

As long as you are living
it is your birthday. And, maybe,
even if you are not.

So, happy birthday.

The white cloth is on the table.
The August light looks like early May.
And dawn looks a little bit like dusk.
And you look a little bit like me
and I a little bit like you.

Our eyes are the only eyes we will ever have.

A ribbon of cloud darkens
above an ocean.
Everything is happening.

The moment is here,
it has always been here.
It is yours and beautiful in every direction.

Inward too, within us forever,
a shadow leaning all the way back.

And yet, you live where I live,
where sometimes
all we see is violence,
where the news is bad news,
and it's not that the children
are having children,

it's that they are being
let of blood, found
slit and burned, tied to posts
wearing their uniforms.

Isn't it awful,
but aren't we thankful?
Aren't our friends here with gifts?

Isn't the grove alive?
Don't the deer step into our lawns,
onto our closely kept grass?

What is it we expected?
What is it we expected to understand?

I wanted to begin by saying I'm sorry,

not so much for being alive,
but for living.

Maybe you think that's weak,
I don't know.
I can only tell you how I feel.

The houses in the neighborhood
seem to be waiting.

April is invisible.
All the months are invisible.

Whatever moon you see,
call it your own.

It's the only moon you will ever have.

I do know you can listen
to the waves breaking
and not to the ones that have broken,

that the definitions are just ideas,
and purpose is in the living.

I know you
and want to keep knowing you.

At night, sometimes, before I give myself
to the quiet revelry of sleep,
before I open its envelope
and see the light of its kingdom,

I think your face must be different
than the one I see.

I have forgotten what you told me

as we lay on the ground,
but remember the colors you wore.

You are not an age,
but a distance from your birth.

I miss you.
I drove to the sea, arrived at dusk
to hear all the gray tearing at the shore
before I saw it turn thin and white.

The day unfurling
out of its husk. The day,
with all its chance and change,

with its nothing twice,
with no one other
than ourselves, is coming.

Red star. Blue heart.

Happy birthday.

ABOUT THE AUTHOR

Carl Adamshick's first collection, *Curses and Wishes*, won
the Walt Whitman Award in 2010, and was published
by Louisiana State University the following year. He is
cofounder of Tavern Books, a nonprofit publisher of poetry.
He lives in Portland, Oregon.

ACKNOWLEDGMENTS

Some of these poems appeared in the *Missouri Review, Narrative, ZYZZYVA*, and online at the *Rumpus* and Poets.org.

Titles in the Carnegie Mellon University Press Classic Contemporaries Series 1989-2019

Carl Adamshick
Saint Friend

Jon Anderson
In Sepia
Death & Friends

Peter Balakian
Sad Days of Light

Aliki Barnstone
Madly in Love

Marvin Bell
The Escape into You
Stars Which See, Stars Which Do
  Not See

Catherine Bowman
1-800-Hot-Ribs

Michael Casey
Obscenities

Cyrus Cassells
The Mud Actor

Kelly Cherry
Lovers and Agnostics
Relativity

Andrei Codrescu
License to Carry a Gun

Peter Cooley
The Van Gogh Notebook

James Cummins
The Whole Truth

Deborah Digges
Vesper Sparrows

Stuart Dischell
Good Hope Road

Gregory Djanikian
Falling Deeply into America

Stephen Dobyns
Black Dog, Red Dog

Rita Dove
Museum
The Yellow House on the Corner

Norman Dubie
Alehouse Sonnets

Stephen Dunn
Full of Lust and Good Usage
Not Dancing

Stuart Dybek
Brass Knuckles

Cornelius Eady
Victims of the Latest Dance Craze
You Don't Miss Your Water
The Autobiography of a Jukebox

Peter Everwine
Collecting the Animals

Annie Finch
Eve

Maria Flook
Reckless Wedding

Charles Fort
Town Clock Burning

Tess Gallagher
Instructions to the Double

Brendan Galvin
Early Returns

Amy Gerstler
Bitter Angel

David Mura
After We Lost Our Way

Carol Muske
Skylight

William Olsen
*The Hand of God and a Few Bright
    Flowers*

Dzvinia Orlowsky
A Handful of Bees

Gregory Orr
Burning the Empty Nests

Greg Pape
Black Branches

Joyce Peseroff
The Hardness Scale

Kevin Prufer
The Finger Bone

William Pitt Root
The Storm and Other Poems

Mary Ruefle
Cold Pluto
The Adamant

Ira Sadoff
Palm Reading in Winter

Jeannine Savard
Snow Water Cove

Tim Seibles
Body Moves

Gladys Schmitt
Sonnets for an Analyst

Dennis Schmitz
We Weep for Our Strangeness

Jane Shore
The Minute Hand
Eye Level

Dave Smith
The Fisherman's Whore
In the House of the Judge

Elizabeth Spires
Swan's Island

Kim Stafford
*A Thousand Friends of Rain: New
    and Selected Poems 1976-1998*

Maura Stanton
Snow on Snow
Cries of Swimmers

Gerald Stern
Lucky Life
Two Long Poems
The Red Coal

James Tate
The Oblivion Ha-Ha
Absences

Jean Valentine
Pilgrims

Ellen Bryant Voigt
The Forces of Plenty
The Lotus Flowers

James Welch
Riding the Earthboy 40

Evan Zimroth
Giselle Considers Her Future